The Illustrated
Happiness Trap

The Illustrated
Happiness Trap

How to Stop Struggling and Start Living

Dr. Russ Harris
& Bev Aisbett

Shambhala
Boulder
2014

Shambhala Publications, Inc.
2129 13th Street
Boulder, Colorado 80302
www.shambhala.com

Published by arrangement with Exisle Publishing Ltd, Wollombi, Australia

14 13 12 11 10 9

Printed in the United States of America

⊗This edition is printed on acid-free paper that meets
the American National Standards Institute Z39.48 Standard.
♻Shambhala Publications makes every effort to print on recycled paper.
For more information please visit www.shambhala.com.

Shambhala Publications is distributed worldwide by
Penguin Random House, Inc., and its subsidiaries.

Designed by IslandBridge

Library of Congress Cataloging-in-Publication Data
Harris, Russ, 1962–
[Happiness trap pocketbook]
The illustrated happiness trap: how to stop struggling
and start living / Dr. Russ Harris & Bev Aisbett.
pages cm
ISBN 978-1-61180-157-6 (pbk.: alk. paper)
1. Happiness. I. Aisbett, Bev. II. Title.
BF575.H27H375 2014
158.1—dc23
2013029005

Contents

Welcome to *The Illustrated Happiness Trap*, an illustrated and simplified version of the international bestseller, *The Happiness Trap*. There are at least three ways you could use this book:

1. As an easy-to-read introduction to Acceptance & Commitment Therapy

This book presents a delightfully easy introduction to the main ideas of Acceptance & Commitment Therapy (better known as ACT). We see it as especially useful for people who are not really into reading traditional self-help books, or for those who are so stressed, anxious, or depressed that reading is difficult. Of course, we hope that you will then go on to read the original book, which explores ACT in far greater depth.

2. As an adjunct to coaching or therapy

If you are seeing a coach or therapist who uses the ACT approach, this book can be a valuable adjunct. You can read chapters ahead of time to prepare for a session, or after a session as a reminder.

3. As a quick refresher course

If it's been a while since you read *The Happiness Trap*, you can use this book as a quick refresher course to remind yourself of the main ideas and exercises.

An Important Message

Simply reading this book will not be enough to make any real difference in your life. You actually will need to do the exercises if you want your life to be richer, fuller, and more meaningful. It is much the same as reading a book on how to play tennis or guitar. Your tennis or guitar skills won't improve simply from reading it; you actually have to do the recommended exercises.

Of course, you can read through the book quickly and then go back and do the exercises, but it's far better to do them as you go.

So, good luck with it all. And remember: life gives most to those who make the most of what life gives.

Cheers
Russ Harris

Introduction

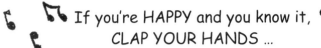 If you're HAPPY and you know it, CLAP YOUR HANDS ...

OH DEAR!

We should be HAPPY, shouldn't we?

That's what the multitude of self-help books out there suggest — just think happy thoughts and you'll be FINE. But trying to be perpetually positive can be downright STRESSFUL!

MY DOG DIED, I LOST MY JOB, MY WIFE LEFT ME ... BUT IT'S ALL *GOOD*!

BUT ISN'T IT *NORMAL* TO BE HAPPY?

You'd think that it would be normal to be happy in the Western world, where we have access to so many of the ingredients to build happiness ...

GOOD HOUSING

MORE & BETTER FOOD

EXCELLENT MEDICAL FACILITIES

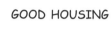

ACCESS TO

EDUCATION

JUSTICE

WELFARE

CLEAN WATER

&

SANITATION

Along with FREEDOM TO

TRAVEL

SPEAK OPENLY

VOTE

But the truth is, on the whole we're NOT happy.
In fact, often we're downright MISERABLE!

Here are some sobering statistics:

1 in 10 has
CLINICAL DEPRESSION

1 in 5 is DEPRESSED
at some time

1 in 4 has or has had an
ADDICTION

30 percent of the adult
population has a recognized
PSYCHOLOGICAL DISORDER

And of all the people you know, almost HALF of these will
SERIOUSLY CONTEMPLATE SUICIDE at some point ...

... and 1 in 10 will actually
ATTEMPT IT!

SO WHY IS IT SO *DIFFICULT* TO BE HAPPY?

TO ANSWER THAT, WE NEED TO GO BACK IN TIME TO SEE HOW OUR MINDS *EVOLVED*!

HANG ON!

WOW!!

HERE'S AN EARLY HUNTER/GATHERER. WHAT DO YOU THINK ARE HIS *NEEDS*?

HMM ... WELL, THE *BASICS* FOR SURVIVAL!

FOOD WATER SHELTER SEX

AND HE HAS AN EVEN *GREATER* PRIORITY!

DON'T GET **KILLED!**

THE BETTER WE WERE ABLE TO ANTICIPATE AND AVOID DANGER, THE BETTER OUR CHANCES OF *SURVIVAL*!

GOOD? BAD? HELPFUL?

TRUE, BUT THERE AREN'T ANY *SABER-TOOTHED TIGERS* IN MY SUBURB! WHAT'S THIS GOT TO DO WITH MODERN-DAY HAPPINESS?

WELL, LOOK AT HOW WE'VE *"EVOLVED"*! COMPARE THE *"DANGERS"* ON OUR ANCESTORS' LIST TO OUR CURRENT PERCEIVED *"DANGERS"* — MOST OF WHICH WON'T EVEN HAPPEN!

SO I GUESS WE'VE JUST EVOLVED TO BE BETTER AT LOOKING FOR *TROUBLE*!

PREDATORS
BAD WEATHER
ILLNESS
LACK OF FOOD OR WATER

MORTGAGE REJECTION *JOB*

EMBARRASSMENT LOSS

WAR

UPSETTING LOVED ONES

BANKRUPTCY

PAYING BILLS **THEFT**

SPEEDING TICKET

Climate Change **POLLUTION**

GETTING CANCER ATTACK

OBESITY DRUGS **STUFF**

WHAT DO YOU THINK WAS THE GREATEST *THREAT* TO SURVIVAL FOR OUR FRIEND HERE?

LET'S SEE ... WELL, BEING *ALONE* WOULD BE DANGEROUS, I GUESS!

YES! WITHOUT THE PROTECTION OF THE TRIBE, HE WOULD BE *EASY PREY*!

SO HOW DOES THIS PLAY OUT IN *MODERN TIMES*?

WE STILL FEAR *REJECTION* AND TRY TO "PROTECT" OURSELVES BY COMPARING OURSELVES TO OTHERS!

AM I *FITTING IN*?

AM I DOING ANYTHING *WRONG*?

AM I AS *GOOD* AS OTHERS?

AND BACK THEN, THERE WAS ONLY A SMALL GROUP TO COMPARE TO!

NOW IT'S *GLOBAL*!

FOR AN AMBITIOUS ANCESTOR THE FORMULA FOR SUCCESS WAS *MORE = BETTER*

WELL THAT SURE HASN'T *CHANGED*!

AND IT SEEMS THAT NO MATTER HOW MUCH WE GET, WE STILL WANT MORE!

YES! OUR MODERN MINDS TEND TO FOCUS ON *LACK* & CREATE DISSATISFACTION!

SO WHAT *IS* THIS HAPPINESS THAT WE KEEP CHASING AFTER?

"The very purpose of life is to seek Happiness."

Dalai Lama

"HAPPINESS" HAS TWO VERY DIFFERENT MEANINGS ...

1.
A GOOD FEELING

Because happiness feels GOOD, we CHASE it, but we find that it doesn't LAST.

And, as we shall see, a life spent chasing after this feeling is not only UNSATISFACTORY but also the harder we try to experience only pleasurable feelings, the more we feel ANXIOUS or DEPRESSED when they elude us.

2.
AN ACTIVE PHILOSOPHY

THIS SECOND DEFINITION INSTEAD FOCUSES ON CREATING A *RICH, FULL & MEANINGFUL* LIFE!

This involves ...

TAKING ACTION ON THE THINGS THAT MATTER TO US

MOVING IN THE DIRECTION OF WHAT WE SEE AS VALUABLE OR WORTHY

ENGAGING FULLY IN WHAT WE DO

IN DOING SO, WE EMBRACE LIFE IN *ALL* ITS COLORS!

But a full human life comes with the FULL RANGE of human emotions.

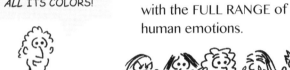

> OF COURSE WE ALL LIKE TO FEEL *GOOD*, BUT DESPERATELY TRYING TO AVOID PAINFUL FEELINGS DOOMS US TO *FAILURE*.

The fact is — life involves PAIN:

LOSS

SEPARATION OR DIVORCE

REJECTION

ILLNESS OR INFIRMITY

THE GOOD NEWS IS ...

You can learn to handle painful feelings by:

► MAKING ROOM FOR THEM

► RISING ABOVE THEM

► CREATING A LIFE WORTH LIVING.

> AND WE'LL SHOW YOU HOW, USING THE PRINCIPLES OF *ACT: ACCEPTANCE AND COMMITMENT THERAPY*.

Chapter 1

Fairytales

... AND THEY LIVED *HAPPILY EVER AFTER* ...

WE'LL ALL LIVE HAPPILY EVER AFTER, WON'T WE MOMMY?

HMMM ...

HAPPY ENDINGS ... we believe that's how life should be, don't we? Is this REALISTIC? Does this fit with your own experience of life?

An expectation that life should turn out "happily ever after" is one of the ways that we find ourselves caught in the **HAPPINESS TRAP**.

LET'S EXPLORE THE FOUR MYTHS WHICH MAKE UP THE *HAPPINESS TRAP* ...

MYTH 1:
HAPPINESS IS THE NATURAL STATE FOR HUMAN BEINGS

Our culture insists that humans are naturally happy. Yet, the scary statistics regarding mental illness in the introduction to this book tell another story.

And aside from diagnosed psychiatric disorders, there are things like:

LONELINESS	SEXUAL PROBLEMS	ILLNESS	WORK STRESS

BULLYING	PREJUDICE	LOW SELF-ESTEEM	CHRONIC ANGER

LACK OF MEANING	MID-LIFE CRISIS	SOCIAL ISOLATION

SO LASTING HAPPINESS IS ACTUALLY QUITE *RARE*, YET MANY OF US HAVE A BELIEF THAT ...

EVERYONE IS HAPPY EXCEPT *ME*!

... A BELIEF THAT CREATES EVEN *GREATER* UNHAPPINESS!

MYTH 2:
IF YOU'RE NOT HAPPY, YOU'RE DEFECTIVE

I MUST
BE REALLY
MESSED UP!

Our society tends to assume that psychological suffering is ABNORMAL: a sign of a WEAKNESS or ILLNESS and a mind that is FAULTY or DEFECTIVE.

YOU SHOULDN'T
BE FEELING SO
ANXIOUS.

OH NO! I MUST BE
MENTALLY ILL!

This means that, when we inevitably experience painful thoughts and feelings, we BEAT UP on ourselves for doing so.

I'M *WEAK*!

I'M *STUPID*!

BUT AS YOU WILL SEE,
YOUR MIND IS JUST
DOING THE JOB IT
HAS *EVOLVED* TO DO!

ACT PRINCIPLE:

THE *NORMAL*
THINKING PROCESSES
OF A *HEALTHY* MIND
NATURALLY CREATE
PSYCHOLOGICAL
SUFFERING!

MYTH 3:
TO CREATE A BETTER LIFE, WE MUST GET RID OF NEGATIVE FEELINGS

The current trend of a "feel-good" society tells us to ELIMINATE "negative" feelings and ACCUMULATE the "positive."

But in reality, the things we value most in life give rise to a whole RANGE of feelings — PLEASANT and UNPLEASANT.

For instance, in a long-term relationship, there may be JOY ...

... but also FRUSTRATION.

Anything that's MEANINGFUL in our lives will bring with it ... both pleasure *and* pain!

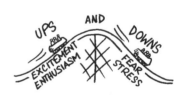

Living life to the full means experiencing UNCOMFORTABLE FEELINGS along the way. Learning how to HANDLE these feelings is essential.

MYTH 4:
YOU SHOULD BE ABLE TO CONTROL WHAT YOU THINK AND FEEL

Many current self-help programs subscribe to this myth by:

REPLACING "NEGATIVE" THOUGHTS WITH "POSITIVE" ONES

DOING AFFIRMATIONS ...   ... OR VISUALIZATIONS

   EVERYTHING IS HUNKY-DORY!   

The basic theme behind these approaches is:

"THINK HAPPY THOUGHTS AND YOU'LL BE HAPPY."

If only life was that SIMPLE! Over one hundred thousand years of evolution tend to override a few affirmations!

Even though you might be able to master positive thinking when you are relatively CALM, negative thoughts will start to creep in again when you feel STRESSED.

ANGER SADNESS INSECURITY GUILT

LA LA LA HAPPY HAPPY

They go away, then they're back. They go away, then they're back — and the battle to keep them at bay can be STRESSFUL in itself!

AARGH! CAN'T BE SAD/ ANGRY/ UPSET!

These four basic myths set us up for a battle we can NEVER WIN.

SO ARE YOU SAYING THAT NEGATIVE THOUGHTS AND FEELINGS ARE *NORMAL*?

YES. LIFE INVOLVES *PAIN*.

THEN HOW DID THESE MYTHS BECOME SO *ENTRENCHED* IN OUR CULTURE?

BECAUSE WE HAVE SO MUCH *CONTROL* OVER THE MATERIAL WORLD WE EXPECT TO HAVE *CONTROL* OVER OUR INTERNAL WORLD, BUT THIS IS *UNREALISTIC*.

TRY THESE EXPERIMENTS AND YOU'LL *SEE*!

1. DON'T THINK ABOUT ICE CREAM FOR 30 SECONDS. DON'T THINK ABOUT ITS COLOR, TEXTURE OR TASTE.

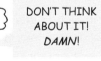

DON'T THINK ABOUT IT! *DAMN*!

2. LOOK AT THIS STAR FOR ONE MINUTE, BUT AS YOU DO, DON'T THINK ABOUT IT!

DAMN!

3. IMAGINE SOMEONE POINTS A GUN AT YOUR HEAD, AND SAYS "YOU MUST FEEL NO ANXIETY — OR I WILL SHOOT YOU!"

I GUESS IT WOULD BE *CURTAINS* FOR ME!

4. CONJURE UP A MEMORY. NOW FORGET IT.

CAN'T.

5. FEEL THE INSIDE OF YOUR MOUTH. NOW MAKE IT NUMB.

I CAN STILL FEEL IT.

From an early age, we are taught that we should be able to CONTROL OUR FEELINGS:

| DON'T CRY | STOP FROWNING | STOP FEELING SORRY FOR YOURSELF | THERE'S NO NEED TO BE SCARED |

And this is REINFORCED as we get older.

| YOU BIG SISSY! | CHILL OUT! | SNAP OUT OF IT! | DON'T BE SUCH A CHICKEN! |

The implication is that you should be able to flick a switch and turn your feelings on or off at WILL.

BUT WHY IS THIS *MYTH* SO COMPELLING?

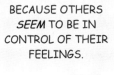

BECAUSE OTHERS *SEEM* TO BE IN CONTROL OF THEIR FEELINGS.

The reality is that most people hide their inner struggles behind a MASK OF COPING ...

WORRY
WORRY
WORRY

NO *WORRIES* *MATE*!

... and this false front adds to the ILLUSION of CONTROL.

Chapter 2

Vicious cycles

What's happening in your life?

I HAVE RELATIONSHIP PROBLEMS!

I HATE MY JOB!

I'M LONELY.

I HAVE HEALTH ISSUES.

I FEEL REJECTED.

I'VE LOST CONFIDENCE!

I'M AN ADDICT!

I'M IN FINANCIAL CRISIS!

I'M JUST STUCK!

I'M ANXIOUS!

I'M DEPRESSED!

WELL I HAVE EVERYTHING I NEED BUT I'M UNHAPPY.

Whatever the problem is, it gives rise to UNPLEASANT THOUGHTS and FEELINGS which you try to GET RID OF.

The more you try to GET RID OF, AVOID, or ESCAPE feelings, the BIGGER they become.

ALCOHOL HELPS ME COPE WITH MY *SOCIAL ANXIETY*!

OH *NO*! DID I REALLY DO *THAT* LAST NIGHT?

AND I SPENT ALL THAT *MONEY*!

I'M TOO *ASHAMED* TO FACE ANYONE!

CHOCOLATE *CHEERS ME UP*!

TEMPORARILY!

YOU'RE ALWAYS WORKING! WHY DON'T YOU STAY HOME WITH *ME*?

IT'S SO *TENSE* AT HOME!

WHERE ARE YOU?!

I HAD TO DO *OVERTIME* AGAIN!

We have two main ways of trying to avoid painful thoughts and feelings: FIGHT or FLIGHT.

FIGHT

Trying to fight against unwanted thoughts/ feelings by:

SUPPRESSION

You forcefully push away unwanted thoughts or unwanted feelings deep inside.

ARGUING WITH YOURSELF

YOU'RE A FAILURE!

NO I'M NOT!

You attempt to challenge and disprove negative thoughts.

FLIGHT

Running away or hiding from unwanted thoughts/ feelings by:

HIDING/ESCAPING

You avoid situations in which you feel uncomfortable.

DISTRACTION

You focus on something else to avoid unwanted thoughts and feelings.

TAKING CHARGE

SNAP OUT OF IT!
STAY CALM!
CHEER UP!

You try to force yourself
to feel better.

SELF-BULLYING

IDIOT!
DON'T BE SO
PATHETIC!

You beat yourself up for
having these thoughts/
feelings.

ZONING OUT/ NUMBING

You make yourself
"unconscious" to the
thoughts/feelings.

PILLS AND DRUGS

You use medication,
alcohol, or drugs to
escape the pain.

BUT WHAT'S
WRONG WITH
THESE THINGS
IF THEY HELP
YOU TO COPE?

NOTHING —
IF YOU USE
THEM ...

▶ IN MODERATION

▶ WHEN THEY CAN
ACTUALLY WORK

▶ IF THEY DON'T
STOP YOU DOING
THE THINGS YOU
VALUE.

For example,
DISTRACTING YOURSELF
after an argument or a
tough day can be helpful ...

I NEED SOME
TIME OUT!

... but if you spend ALL
NIGHT distracting yourself
you'll miss out on LIFE!

Any method to avoid pain, if used excessively will create
GREATER PROBLEMS:

AAH!
CHOCOLATE!

OOH AH!
DIABETES!

I'LL TAKE MY MIND
OFF THIS *EXAM
STRESS*!

Trying to BURY deep pain doesn't make it DISAPPEAR!

Avoiding painful feelings can stop you doing what you VALUE:

A simple RELAXATION TECHNIQUE may be enough to ease a stressful day at WORK ...

RELAX AND BREATHE ...

... but it won't do much for OUTRIGHT TERROR!

RELAX?! ARE YOU *KIDDING*?!

AND WHILE YOU MIGHT BE ABLE TO SIMPLY *IGNORE* A MESSY ROOM ...

... IT'S HARD TO IGNORE A SINISTER LUMP!

SO HOW DOES THAT FIT WITH THE *HAPPINESS* TRAP?

THE TRAP IS THAT TRYING TO AVOID PAINFUL FEELINGS IS MOSTLY *INEFFECTIVE* ...

▶ IT TAKES A LOT OF TIME AND ENERGY

▶ WE FEEL INADEQUATE WHEN THE UNWANTED THOUGHTS/FEELINGS COME BACK

▶ IT OFTEN HAS LONG-TERM COSTS TO WELLBEING.

... AND YOU END UP IN A LOOP WHERE THE MORE YOU TRY TO AVOID PAIN THE *WORSE* YOU FEEL!

TRY TO AVOID OR GET RID OF THEM

PAINFUL THOUGHTS AND FEELINGS

EVEN MORE PAIN

TRY EVEN HARDER TO AVOID

THIS IS KNOWN AS *"EXPERIENTIAL AVOIDANCE."*

WHAT'S THAT MEAN?

THE ONGOING ATTEMPT TO *AVOID* OR *GET RID* OF UNWANTED THOUGHTS/FEELINGS ...

... NO MATTER THE *COST*!

BUT THE *HARDER* YOU TRY THE *WORSE* YOU FEEL, SO ROUND AND ROUND IT GOES!

38

AND *VOILA!* YOU'RE *TRAPPED!*

You find unwanted thoughts and feelings unpleasant ...

... so you are worse off than when you started!

SAD ANGRY UNLOVABLE HURT SHAME *NOOO!*

So you try to **ESCAPE** them ...

START HERE

... by retreating to your **HAPPY PLACE** ...

BLEW IT! STUPID! WRONG! BAD! LOSER!

SLAM! LA LA LA HAPPY! HAPPY!

... and now you find that your Happy Place has bred even more ...

THE HAPPINESS TRAP

ALL IS WELL OMMM

HUH? OH NO! BAD

... but your **HAPPY PLACE** is built from temporary and often toxic things ...

... which are not strong enough to keep them out forever ...

EXERCISE

List the thoughts & feelings you'd like to get rid of. Now list every method you've used so far to avoid or get rid of them (e.g. drugs, alcohol, food, procrastination, avoiding difficult situations, etc). Did these strategies work in the long term? What was the cost?

WHAT ABOUT DOING GOOD *WORKS* AND GIVING TO OTHERS? DOESN'T THAT BRING *HAPPINESS*?

IT CAN — BUT IT WON'T BE *SATISFYING* IF YOUR MAIN AIM IS TO *AVOID* THOUGHTS AND FEELINGS SUCH AS ....

I'M A BAD FATHER!

I'M SELFISH!

NOBODY LIKES ME.

I'M NOT APPRECIATED FOR WHAT I DO!

IF I GIVE THEY'LL LIKE ME!

NEGATIVE THOUGHTS

FEELING INADEQUATE

FEARING REJECTION

DOING SOMETHING TO AVOID PAIN IS *UNFULFILLING*. MUCH BETTER TO DO IT BECAUSE IT'S *MEANINGFUL*!

Consider running through a forest. You can run through a forest to MEET YOUR LOVER.

You can run through a forest to ESCAPE A BEAR.

When we do any activity primarily to escape or avoid something unwanted, it is usually unfulfilling, because it feels like we are on the run from something, rather than doing something meaningful. Of course, we are not usually on the run from wild animals, but rather from painful thoughts and feelings.

Likewise you can go to the gym to look after and TAKE CARE OF YOUR BODY.

Or you can go to the gym to ESCAPE UNPLEASANT THOUGHTS OR FEELINGS.

You'll hear a lot of ADVICE on how to IMPROVE YOUR LIFE:

But be warned: if you start doing any of these things primarily to ESCAPE or AVOID unpleasant feelings, it probably won't be rewarding. Better to do things because they are genuinely important and meaningful, rather than to try to avoid pain.

The basics of ACT

ACT — **ACCEPTANCE and COMMITMENT THERAPY** — is based on two main principles: "mindfulness" and "values." These principles work together to help you:

▶ **EFFECTIVELY HANDLE PAINFUL THOUGHTS AND FEELINGS**

▶ **CREATE A RICH, FULL, AND MEANINGFUL LIFE.**

Mindfulness is a special mental state of AWARENESS and OPENNESS. Mindfulness involves three skills:

SKILL 1: DEFUSION

When you learn to defuse painful and unpleasant thoughts, self-limiting beliefs, and self-criticism, they have less influence over you.

SKILL 2: EXPANSION

This means making room for painful thoughts and feelings and allowing them to flow through you, without getting swept away by them.

SKILL 3: CONNECTION

This means living fully in the present instead of dwelling on the past or worrying about the future.

DEFUSION, EXPANSION, AND *CONNECTION* ARE TOGETHER KNOWN AS *MINDFULNESS.*

Values are your heart's deepest desires for how you want to behave as a human being; what you want to STAND FOR in life.

In *ACT*, you use values to give life MEANING, PURPOSE, and DIRECTION.

And you translate values into COMMITTED ACTION: you do what really matters to you!

ACT is a scientifically proven method to help you build a RICHER, FULLER, and more MEANINGFUL life.

Are you ready to GET MOVING? Let's go!

ONE STEP AT A TIME!

Chapter 4

The great storyteller

 NOW WE'RE GOING TO LOOK AT HOW TO HANDLE OUR *THOUGHTS*.

 WHAT *ARE* THOUGHTS EXACTLY?

 THOUGHTS ARE BASICALLY *WORDS*.

 WORDS?

We use words in different settings ...

| WORDS ON A PAGE ARE CALLED **TEXT**: | WORDS SPOKEN OUT LOUD ARE CALLED **SPEECH**: | AND WORDS INSIDE OUR HEAD ARE CALLED **THOUGHTS**: |

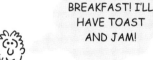

The quick brown fox jumps over the lazy dog.

YAKKITY YAK

BLAH BLAH BLAH

Thoughts can also be IMAGES:

WORDS

IMAGE

BREAKFAST! I'LL HAVE TOAST AND JAM!

But please don't confuse THOUGHTS with FEELINGS or SENSATIONS — which we feel in the BODY.

 GURGLE

47

We'll explore FEELINGS and SENSATIONS later. Let's stick with THOUGHTS for now.

THOUGHTS — TELL US ABOUT LIFE & HOW TO LIVE IT ...

... HOW WE ARE OR SHOULD BE AND WHAT TO AVOID.

DO THIS
DO THAT

LIKE THIS
DON'T LIKE
THAT

What we tend to forget is that thoughts are just words which constitute our stories.

These can be TRUE stories called **FACTS** ...

... or FALSE stories.

NO-ONE
EVER
LIKES ME!!!

IT'S MY
DAY OFF!

But most stories are based on how we see life according to our ...

or what we want to do with our lives:

OPINIONS
ATTITUDES
JUDGMENTS
IDEALS
BELIEFS
MORALS

PLANS
STRATEGIES
GOALS
WISHES
VALUES

THE HUMAN MIND IS LIKE A STORYTELLING MACHINE. ALL IT WANTS IS OUR *ATTENTION*!

BLAH, BLAH, BLAH, STORY, STORY, STORY, GIVE ME YOUR ATTENTION!

BUT IF WE GET TOO *CAUGHT UP* IN THESE STORIES, IT CREATES PROBLEMS:

BAD THINGS WILL HAPPEN!

I'M NOT *GOOD ENOUGH.*

HOW *DARE* THEY?!

I *CAN'T* DO IT!

WHEN A STORY *DOMINATES* US — WHEN IT CAPTURES OUR FULL ATTENTION OR DICTATES HOW WE BEHAVE — WE REFER TO THIS AS *FUSION*.

NOW HERE'S AN *AMAZING FACT* ...

NEWS FLASH!

NO THOUGHT IS PROBLEMATIC IN AND OF ITSELF. OUR THOUGHTS ONLY BECOME PROBLEMATIC IF WE "FUSE" WITH THEM!

REALLY?

SURE! IN A MOMENT YOU'LL SEE THAT NO MATTER HOW *NEGATIVE* A THOUGHT IS, IT'S ONLY PROBLEMATIC IF YOU *FUSE* WITH IT!

I DON'T UNDERSTAND!

THIS WILL MAKE IT CLEARER. JOT DOWN SOME OF YOUR NEGATIVE THOUGHTS ON A SHEET OF PAPER.

OKAY.

NOW HOLD THE PAPER IN FRONT OF YOUR FACE AND GET ALL ABSORBED IN THOSE WORDS.

WHILE YOU'RE ALL CAUGHT UP IN THESE THOUGHTS YOU ARE *CUT OFF* OR *DISCONNECTED* FROM THE THINGS THAT MAKE LIFE *MEANINGFUL*.

AND WHILE YOU'RE HOLDING ON TIGHTLY TO THESE *THOUGHTS*, IT'S HARD TO DO THE THINGS THAT MAKE YOUR LIFE *WORK*!

IMAGINE TRYING TO *COOK DINNER, DRIVE A CAR, CUDDLE A BABY*, OR *WATCH A MOVIE* WHEN YOU'RE DOING *THIS*!

WHEN WE *FUSE* WITH OUR THOUGHTS THEY SEEM TO BE ...

▶ **THE TRUTH**	You should BELIEVE THEM!
▶ **IMPORTANT**	You should give them your FULL ATTENTION!
▶ **ORDERS**	You must OBEY them!
▶ **GREAT ADVICE**	You should do what they SUGGEST!
▶ **THREATS**	They are DANGEROUS or FRIGHTENING.

NOW TUCK THAT SHEET OF PAPER UNDER YOUR ARM ...

... AND NOTICE THAT NOW YOU CAN *CONNECT* AND *ENGAGE* WITH THE THINGS THAT MAKE LIFE *MEANINGFUL*!

WHEN YOU DO THIS WITH YOUR THOUGHTS WE CALL IT *DEFUSION*.

CAN YOU SHOW ME *HOW*?

SURE. FIRST, BRING TO MIND A *NEGATIVE SELF-JUDGMENT* ...

I'M *USELESS*!

... NOW *FUSE* WITH IT — *BELIEVE* IT AS MUCH AS YOU CAN.

I'M *USELESS*!

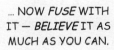

53

NOW INSERT THIS PHRASE IN
FRONT OF IT — "I'M HAVING
THE THOUGHT THAT ..."

*I'M HAVING THE
THOUGHT THAT
I'M USELESS!*

EXERCISE

Pick an upsetting thought, and silently repeat it, putting these words in front of it: "I'm having the thought that ..."

Now try it again with this phrase: "*I notice I'm having the thought that ...*"

Can you feel the thought lose some of its impact?

You can use this simple defusion technique to unhook yourself from any thought, whether true or false — so please play around it.

When we defuse from our thoughts we realize they:

▶ are nothing more or less than WORDS and PICTURES

▶ may or may not be TRUE (we don't have to BELIEVE them)

▶ may or may not be IMPORTANT (we pay attention only if they're helpful)

▶ are not ORDERS (we don't have to obey!)

▶ may or may not be WISE — we don't have to follow the advice

▶ are never actual THREATS, no matter how negative.

SO LET'S *DEFUSE* ANOTHER TROUBLESOME THOUGHT. GOT ONE?

YEP!

I'M A LOSER!

NOW IN YOUR MIND SING IT TO THE TUNE OF *HAPPY BIRTHDAY*!

I'M A L-O-S-E-R I'M A L-O-S-E-R

WHAT HAPPENED?

IT JUST SEEMS LIKE WORDS IN A SONG AND DOESN'T BOTHER ME!

EXERCISE

Pick a thought that bothers you, and silently sing it to the tune "Happy Birthday."

What happens when you do that?

Notice that you haven't tried to challenge it, avoid it, or get rid of it. But hopefully you can now see it for what it is: nothing more or less than a string of words.

The mind LOVES its STORIES! Unfortunately many of these stories are UNHELPFUL.

It's normal for about 80 percent of our thoughts to have some negative content. The trouble arises only when we FUSE with these thoughts and when we let them DOMINATE us. This feeds:

INSECURITY   ANXIETY   DEPRESSION

ANGER   LOW SELF-ESTEEM   SELF-DOUBT

Some psychological approaches advise you to:

▶ check the FACTS and correct MENTAL ERRORS

▶ make the story more POSITIVE

▶ tell yourself a better STORY

▶ DISTRACT yourself

▶ PUSH the story away

▶ DEBATE the truth of the story.

But these strategies rarely work in the long run.

NEGATIVE STORIES AREN'T THE PROBLEM! THE PROBLEM IS GETTING *CAUGHT UP IN THEM* OR LETTING THEM *DICTATE* YOUR *ACTIONS*.

Just like those tabloid stories — you can BUY INTO them ...

THAT'S *AWFUL!*

STAR DIES...
OF EMBARRASSMENT

... or NOT!

BLIMEY! WHAT WILL THEY *DREAM UP* NEXT?

Trying to CHANGE, AVOID, or GET RID OF a story is often INEFFECTIVE. Instead, simply name it for what it IS!

THIS IS A *STORY*!

Try naming your own stories and see they are nothing more than WORDS.

THE "I'M A LOSER" STORY	THE "I'M FAT" STORY	THE "I CAN'T COPE" STORY	THE "I'M UNLOVABLE" STORY

Please try these defusion techniques with your own thoughts.

For example, if you have lots of thoughts about being "not good enough" then whenever they show up, say to yourself, "Aha! There it is again! The 'Not Good Enough' story."

If you like, you can also add, with a sense of humor, "Thanks, mind!"

Chapter 5

True blues

ACT: WHAT'S IMPORTANT IS NOT
WHETHER OR NOT A THOUGHT IS TRUE
BUT
**WHETHER OR NOT IT HELPS YOU
TO HOLD ON TO IT!**

EXAMPLE 1

UNHELPFUL		**HELPFUL**

I'M
INCOMPETENT!

I COULD ASK
FOR HELP.

Does holding on
to that thought
when it appears
IMPROVE your
performance?

**Belittling/
Unsettling**

**Expanding skills
and knowledge**

EXAMPLE 2

UNHELPFUL		**HELPFUL**

I'M A LUMP
OF LARD!

I'LL GO FOR
A WALK!

Does holding on
to that thought
when it appears
make you want
to LOOK AFTER
yourself?

**Blaming,
demoralizing**

**Making healthier
choices!**

EVEN IF IT'S *TRUE*!

BUT I REALLY *HAVE* BLOWN ALL MY SAVINGS!

Does getting caught in these thoughts help you COPE?

NO, I JUST FEEL MORE DEPRESSED AND THINK *WORSE* THOUGHTS!

PATHETIC!

LOSER!

NOW LET'S TAKE A LOOK AT THE SO-CALLED "IMPOSTER SYNDROME"!

John does his job well. He's EFFICIENT and COMPETENT.

But his mind has OTHER IDEAS!

I'M A *FRAUD*. I'M JUST *LUCKY* THAT IT WORKED OUT. I'M SURE TO *BLOW IT* AND BE FOUND OUT!

With the IMPOSTER SYNDROME, John is paying more attention to his overcritical thoughts ...

... than the direct experience.

YOU DON'T KNOW WHAT YOU'RE DOING!

YOU'RE SCREWING IT UP!

YEAH, *RIGHT*!

THAT'S *PERFECT* JOHN!

THANKS.

John has been "hooked" by the "I'm Incompetent" story. He needs to unhook himself and turn his attention to what's REALLY happening.

EXERCISES

1. NOT TAKING A THOUGHT SERIOUSLY

Imagine the thought on a computer screen.

Play around with the font and the color.

2. THANKING YOUR MIND

When the same old stories come up,

MY LIFE'S *HOPELESS*.

say them to yourself with a sense of humor!

AHA! HERE IT IS AGAIN! THE *"MY LIFE'S HOPELESS"* STORY!

IS THAT *RIGHT*? THANKS FOR SHARING!

OR simply —

THANKS MIND!

3. SILLY VOICES

Pick a recurring self-judgment.

I'M STUPID!

Silently say it to yourself in the voice of a cartoon or movie character.

I'M STHTOOPID!

4. KIDS COMIC BOOK

I CAN'T DO IT!

Imagine your thought inside a thought bubble in a comic book.

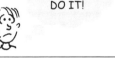

Again, notice that you have not tried to avoid or change the thought, you've just seen it for what it is — WORDS.

BUT I HAVE *TERMINAL CANCER*! IF I HAVE A THOUGHT THAT I'LL BE DEAD SOON, THAT'S BOTH *TRUE* AND *SERIOUS*!

YES, BUT IS IT *HELPFUL* TO GET ENTANGLED IN THOSE THOUGHTS? DO YOU WANT TO SPEND THE TIME YOU HAVE LEFT STUCK INSIDE YOUR THOUGHTS OR DOING THINGS THAT *MATTER*?

I'M SORRY BUT I CAN'T DO THE SILLY VOICES FOR THIS. IT'S TOO *PAINFUL*!

That's fine; pick another technique that works for you.

HOW LONG DO I HAVE TO DO THESE?

Until you are able to defuse your thoughts quickly.

DEFUSION GUIDELINES

▶ See the thoughts for what they are — nothing more or less than WORDS.

▶ Don't EXPECT anything. Just observe what happens.

▶ The thoughts may go or not. The technique may work sometimes but not at others.

▶ You're HUMAN — your thoughts will snare you again. But now you know how you can quickly unhook yourself.

▶ Like any skill, the more you practice the better you get.

NO TECHNIQUE IS *FOOLPROOF*. EVEN DEFUSION HAS ITS STICKING POINTS — LET'S EXAMINE AND UNSTICK THEM.

Chapter 6

Troubleshooting defusion

I TRIED DEFUSION AND IT DOESN'T *WORK*.

YOU MEAN YOU STAYED *ENTANGLED* IN THE STORY?

NO. I UNHOOKED MYSELF BUT I STILL FELT *ANXIOUS*!

BUT DEFUSION IS NOT A WAY TO *CONTROL* YOUR FEELINGS!

THE PURPOSE OF DEFUSION IS ...

... to see your thoughts as words and unhook yourself — so you can do the things that matter and engage in them fully.

BUT I DON'T *LIKE* FEELING ANXIOUS!

OF *COURSE*! NOBODY DOES!

But the more you struggle with painful feelings, the bigger they get! Later in the book we'll show you a new way to handle them!

HMPH! I DID THAT DEFUSION TECHNIQUE BUT THE THOUGHTS DIDN'T *GO AWAY*.

SOMETIMES THEY *GO*, SOMETIMES THEY STAY. WE'RE NOT TRYING TO GET *RID* OF THE THOUGHTS — JUST TO *UNHOOK* OURSELVES.

BUT SHOULDN'T I TRY TO THINK MORE *POSITIVELY*?

THE ISSUE IS NOT WHETHER YOUR THOUGHTS ARE *POSITIVE* OR *NEGATIVE*. THE QUESTION IS THIS ...

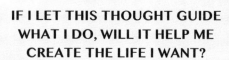

IF I LET THIS THOUGHT GUIDE WHAT I DO, WILL IT HELP ME CREATE THE LIFE I WANT?

BUT POSITIVE THOUGHTS ARE ALWAYS *HELPFUL*, AREN'T THEY?

WELL, A DRUNK DRIVER MAY THINK HE'S COMPETENT TO DRIVE — THAT *IS A* POSITIVE THOUGHT, BUT IS IT *HELPFUL?*

CRASH!

BUT NEGATIVE THOUGHTS ARE *UNHELPFUL* RIGHT?

NOT NECESSARILY! IF A NEGATIVE THOUGHT LEADS TO *POSITIVE* ACTION, IT CAN BE *HELPFUL.*

I MIGHT SCREW UP THE TEST!

I'D BETTER GO DO SOME PREPARATION!

Negative thoughts are not the ENEMY! They are just WORDS and PICTURES floating through your mind. Fight them and you'll be fighting YOURSELF.

SO IS *FUSION* EVER *HELPFUL?*

IT CAN BE!

Planning your future, mentally rehearsing your actions, getting lost in a book can all be HELPFUL types of FUSION.

So when a thought appears, if it's helpful, USE it and if not, DEFUSE it.

Increase your AWARENESS of when and where you fuse, and the sorts of thoughts you tend to fuse with. The aim is to get better at catching yourself doing it, so you can then consciously choose how to act on those thoughts.

And like learning any new skill you'll need to PRACTICE till it becomes more natural to you. Pick ONE or TWO defusion techniques and practice them at every opportunity. AT LEAST 10 times a day but the more the better!

So if at this point your mind says:

IDIOT!

THEN DEFUSE!

STUPID THING TO SAY!

THEN DEFUSE!

MY LIFE SUCKS!

THEN DEFUSE!

IT'S ALL TOO HARD. I CAN'T BE BOTHERED.

And if you're now thinking ...

THANKS MIND!

DEFUSE FROM THAT TOO!

There are TWO PARTS to your MIND:

THE THINKING SELF
is responsible for:
THINKING
PLANNING
JUDGING
COMPARING
CREATING
VISUALIZING
IMAGINING
ANALYZING

THE OBSERVING SELF
is responsible for:
ATTENTION
AWARENESS
CONSCIOUSNESS
NOTICING
OBSERVING

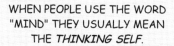

WHEN PEOPLE USE THE WORD
"MIND" THEY USUALLY MEAN
THE *THINKING SELF*.

Life is like a STAGE SHOW and on that stage are all your
THOUGHTS and FEELINGS and everything you can SEE,
HEAR, TOUCH, TASTE, and SMELL.

The OBSERVING
SELF is the part of
you that can step
back and watch the
show.

PRESENTING

Thoughts
Feelings
Touch
Taste
Sight
Hearing
Smell!

Life

The OBSERVING
SELF can zoom in
and take in the DETAILS or zoom out and take in the
WHOLE SHOW — and the show CONTINUALLY CHANGES.

EXERCISE

For 60 SECONDS
close your eyes
and notice what
THOUGHTS
appear ...

The THINKING SELF
creates the thoughts.
The OBSERVING
SELF notices the
thoughts.

Remember — because of the way it evolved, our mind is a bit like RADIO DOOM AND GLOOM:

IT'S RADIO DOOM AND GLOOM!

FIRST LET'S RE-RUN A *HURT FROM THE PAST*, THEN OUR *BUMMER UPDATE* FOLLOWED BY THE *MISERY FORECAST!*

And you can't turn it off! In fact, the HARDER you try, the LOUDER it gets!

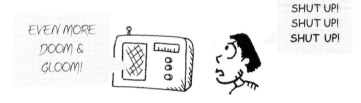

EVEN MORE DOOM & GLOOM!

SHUT UP!
SHUT UP!
SHUT UP!

So if it's broadcasting a HELPFUL story, tune in, and let it guide your actions.

But if it's broadcasting something unhelpful, just let it chatter away in the BACKGROUND.

This doesn't mean you get into a debate with the radio ...

LIFE SUCKS!

OH NO IT *DOESN'T!*

... or try to IGNORE it ...

... you just let it chatter away and ENGAGE in what you're doing.

EXERCISE

Take 10 SLOW, DEEP BREATHS.
Focus fully on the BREATH
and the sensations of BREATHING.

Now let your thoughts
come and go like
PASSING CARS.
Acknowledge them but
stay focused on your
BREATHING.

HMM ...THERE
GO MY
THOUGHTS.

If a thought SNAGS you, gently UNHOOK yourself and REFOCUS on your breathing.

BY PRACTICING THIS TECHNIQUE YOU LEARN HOW TO:

▶ let thoughts come and go
▶ recognize when you've become hooked on a thought
▶ unhook and refocus.

▶ Take what comes — let go of any expectations. If it relaxes you, great but that's a bonus, not the aim.

▶ It doesn't matter how often you get "hooked." Regular unhooking improves your skills.

▶ It's best to practice this for 5–10 minutes, two to three times a day.

NOW REMEMBER, THOUGHTS CAN BE *WORDS* OR *IMAGES*.

We've all conjured up FRIGHTENING IMAGES in our heads ...

and fusing with these images can stop us doing what we VALUE.

NO WAY I'M GETTING ON A *PLANE*!

When we FUSE with these images they seem very REAL or IMPORTANT or SCARY but we can DEFUSE from images, too. Try the following exercises:

EXERCISES

Bring to mind an unpleasant image. Notice how it affects you.

Imagine the image on a TV SCREEN.

Now play around with it — SLOW MOTION, BACKWARDS or change to BLACK AND WHITE.

See? It's just a PICTURE!

Now add a HUMOROUS TITLE or a SILLY VOICEOVER, or ODD MUSIC.

And here in her natural habitat, we see Jenny ...

DUM DUM DA DA!

(Tchaikovsky's 1812 overture)

Or try shifting the LOCATION of the troublesome image. Mentally picture it on a ...

T SHIRT   **CANVAS**   **COMIC**   **POSTAGE STAMP**

If the mental image is still pushing you around, run through these exercises every day till it loosens its grip. You can also adapt previous defusion techniques:

AHA! THE "SCREWED IT UP" STORY!

I'M HAVING AN IMAGE OF ...

I'M HAVING A MEMORY OF ...

NAMING THE STORY   **NAMING THE PICTURE**

THANKS MIND!

or use ...

Here's one final technique (great for moving images).

Change your video clip ...

... to a different GENRE!

CARTOON   **WESTERN**   **SCI FI**   **SOAP OPERA**

THE AIM IS TO *UNHOOK* — NOT TO GET *RID* OF THEM!

WHY?

BECAUSE THEY WILL COME BACK AGAIN AND AGAIN AND FIGHTING THEM IS *HARD WORK*!

REMEMBER — SOMETIMES THESE TECHNIQUES WILL UNHOOK YOU AND SOMETIMES NOT. TAKE WHAT COMES.

Chapter 7

Demons in the boat

Imagine you are in a boat far out to SEA ...

... and below deck are a bunch of demons which are EMOTIONS, THOUGHTS, FEELINGS, and URGES.

If you keep DRIFTING AIMLESSLY they stay below, but as you near land they clamber on deck and OVERWHELM you.

So you make a DEAL.

I'LL KEEP DRIFTING IF YOU STAY BELOW.

OKAY.

But drifting is not FUN.

ANXIOUS BORED LONELY

I HATE THIS!

Besides, other ships are happily landing. Why not YOURS?

But if you try to land, the demons will RESURFACE! WHAT TO DO?

You could try to throw the demons OVERBOARD ...

... but then no one would be steering and you might SINK.

And besides, there are TOO MANY to fight off.

But take a GOOD LOOK at those demons in BROAD DAYLIGHT and you'll discover that they're noisy and ugly but they can't actually HARM you.

GROWL!

GRUMP!

And once you get used to them they're not really THAT scary.

And you'll see they're much SMALLER than you thought!

They may never be cute and cuddly but they no longer have POWER over you.

YOU CAN'T CONTROL ME!

So now you can head to shore and do the things you LIKE!

Your demons love to pop up when you try new things but they can't STOP you!

Ask yourself:

▶ How would I act differently if my demons were no longer a problem?

▶ What activities would I start (or continue)?

▶ What would I do, if fear wasn't a barrier?

▶ What would I stand for, if fear couldn't stop me?

(Are troublesome thoughts or images popping up for you? If so, you know how to defuse!)

Now let's explore the scariest demons of all — **PAINFUL EMOTIONS**.

SO WHAT *ARE EMOTIONS?*

WELL SCIENTIFICALLY SPEAKING THEY:

▶ originate in the mid-brain

▶ involve complex changes in your body.

These changes prepare us for action and lead to a TENDENCY to act in a certain way.

HERE'S SOMEONE EXPERIENCING A STRONG EMOTION — LIKE ANXIETY.

PHYSICAL SENSATIONS

Fast, shallow breathing

Increased heart rate

Sweating

Churning stomach

Urge to run

ACTION TENDENCY

Talk rapidly

Fidget

Pace up and down

NOTICE THE USE OF THE WORD *TENDENCY* WHICH MEANS AN *INCLINATION*!

SO WE *TEND* TO BUT WE DON'T *HAVE* TO?

Emotions are made up of: WORDS and IMAGES in your head and SENSATIONS and FEELINGS in your body.

You can feel ANGRY but act CALM.

You may have a TENDENCY to shout or lash out.

But you don't HAVE TO. You can choose OTHERWISE.

You may have felt fear ... and a TENDENCY to run ...

GULP!

... but you chose NOT TO.

But though you may not have direct control over your FEELINGS ...

... you can directly control your ACTIONS.

YIKES!

DON'T RUN! BACK AWAY SLOWLY!

THE IDEA THAT EMOTIONS CONTROL ACTIONS IS A POWERFUL *ILLUSION*!

When you feel strong emotions it may SEEM as though the emotion is causing your actions.

But with practice, you can control how you act, even when feeling very strong emotions.

Even when you're FURIOUS you can still ...

▶ stand still
▶ speak softly
▶ drink water
▶ go to the toilet.

Emotions are like the weather — ever changing and always present.

MILD  PLEASANT   INTENSE UNPLEASANT

PREDICTABLE

Some people are very in touch with and can express their feelings ...

I FEEL ANXIOUS AND AGITATED.

UNEXPECTED

... while others are more disconnected and have difficulty accessing their feelings.

I DUNNO, I FEEL OKAY I GUESS.

There are THREE PHASES in the creation of an emotion:

1 A significant event occurs either **INTERNALLY (e.g. a thought)**

I'M BAD.

or

EXTERNALLY

and your brain registers this as IMPORTANT ...

2 ... and does an EVALUATION  **? GOOD? BAD?**

... and prepares you for APPROPRIATE ACTION.

 **STAY? GO?**

3 The mind then tells a STORY about the experience ...

FRUSTRATING?
JOYOUS?
SAD?
EXCITING?
GUILTY?

THIS
IS
FUN!

THIS
IS
AWFUL!

... which others may or may not SHARE.

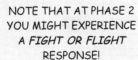

NOTE THAT AT PHASE 2 YOU MIGHT EXPERIENCE A *FIGHT OR FLIGHT* RESPONSE!

WHAT'S THAT?

To save yourself you either stand and FIGHT the woolly mammoth ...

... or take FLIGHT!

Our minds have evolved to look for danger EVERYWHERE ...

| A MOODY SPOUSE | A BIG MORTGAGE | A CONTROLLING BOSS | OR EVEN A FRIGHTENING THOUGHT! |

The fight or flight response triggers unpleasant or negative feelings.

GUILT

FEAR

However, if our brain registers the event as good then pleasant positive feelings are triggered.

JOY

PLEASURE

DELIGHT

But NEGATIVE and POSITIVE are just LABELS for what are simply FEELINGS.

WELL I'D STILL PREFER THE *POSITIVE* ONES!

OF *COURSE*! BUT MAKING THAT PREFERENCE INTO AN "ABSOLUTE MUST" CREATES PROBLEMS.

SO LET'S LOOK AT A NEW WAY TO HANDLE PAINFUL FEELINGS.

Chapter 8

Drop the struggle

Most of us readily buy into STORIES about painful emotions such as:

ANGER
GUILT
SHAME
FEAR
EMBARRASSMENT
AND ANXIETY
ARE NEGATIVE
EMOTIONS.

WHICH
ARE *BAD*
DANGEROUS
IRRATIONAL
AND A SIGN OF
WEAKNESS.

AND SHOW
I *HAVE*
PSYCHOLOGICAL
DEFECTS.

THEY'LL
DAMAGE MY
HEALTH.

PEOPLE SHOULD
HIDE THEIR
FEELINGS.

THEY SHOW
A LACK OF
CONTROL.

I MUST
KEEP MY
EMOTIONS
UNDER
CONTROL.

WOMEN
SHOULDN'T
GET *ANGRY*.

MEN
SHOULDN'T
FEEL *AFRAID*.

Your outlook on expressing emotion is heavily influenced by your CHILDHOOD PROGRAMMING. Negative emotions may have been ...

SUPPRESSED

IF ALLOWED, COULD HAVE BEEN FRIGHTENING

EXERCISE

Take note of your childhood programming about EMOTIONS.

1. What messages were you given?
2. Which emotions were you told were desirable or undesirable?
3. What were you told about the best way to handle emotions?
4. What emotions did your family freely express? Suppress? Frown upon? Hide?
5. With which emotions were your family comfortable? Uncomfortable?
6. How did the adults handle their own emotions?
7. How did they react to your emotions?
8. What did you learn from observing this as you grew?
9. What ideas do you still retain from your programming?

JUDGING OUR EMOTIONS

We tend to judge emotions according to how they FEEL.

BAD   GOOD

Unpleasant
Don't want

Pleasant
Want more

ACT — let go of judging and see them as what they are:

▶ Constantly changing SENSATIONS moving through your body.

▶ No emotion is "GOOD" or "BAD."

▶ An emotion may be PAINFUL or PLEASANT but if we FUSE with the thought that it's BAD, we will struggle with it and make it WORSE.

MY FAMILY DIDN'T OPENLY EXPRESS LOVE AND AFFECTION. I FEEL *UNCOMFORTABLE* DOING SO.

BUT DOES THAT MAKE THESE FEELINGS *BAD*?

WELL I *HATE* FEELING ANXIOUS!

OF *COURSE*! IT'S UNPLEASANT! *NO ONE* ENJOYS IT!

Your mind WILL judge your feelings but you can DEFUSE from these judgments. Here are some examples of DEFUSION TECHNIQUES you can use:

I CAN'T STAND THIS FEELING!

I'M HAVING A THOUGHT THAT I CAN'T STAND THIS FEELING.

THIS IS *AWFUL*!

I'M *NOTICING THE JUDGMENT* THAT THIS ANXIETY IS AWFUL.

Judging ADDS to emotional discomfort and so does ...

REVIEWING   REHASHING   SEARCHING

WHY AM I FEELING LIKE THIS?   WHAT HAVE I DONE TO *DESERVE* THIS?   WHY AM I LIKE THIS?

Reviewing all your PROBLEMS creates the illusion that your life is nothing BUT problems.

Rehashing all your "CRIMES" to explain this "PUNISHMENT" leads to SELF-BLAME.

Searching your life history for someone to BLAME can lead to anger, resentment, and hopelessness.

WHAT'S *WRONG* WITH ME?   I CAN'T HANDLE IT.   I SHOULDN'T FEEL LIKE THIS!   I WISH I DIDN'T FEEL LIKE THIS.

This is another review of all your FAULTS and FLAWS.

Your mind is feeding you a DISEMPOWERING STORY.

This is the mind ARGUING with itself.

Wishing it wasn't like this doesn't change the REALITY.

ASK YOURSELF: IF I HOLD ON TO THESE THOUGHTS, IS THAT *HELPFUL*? DO THEY MAKE IT *EASIER* OR *HARDER* TO HANDLE THE PAIN?

When we feel painful feelings we naturally do what we can to AVOID or GET RID OF them.

But often the things that give us RELIEF in the SHORT TERM ...  ... make our life WORSE in the LONG TERM.

SO HOW DO WE *COPE* WITH PAINFUL FEELINGS?

WE LEARN A SKILL CALLED "EXPANSION."

In order to understand EXPANSION look at some words that describe FEELING BAD:

TENSION — being stretched or stressed

STRESS — subject to strain or pressure

STRAIN — to shock beyond proper limits.

In other words — these terms describe being pulled apart or STRETCHED BEYOND OUR LIMITS.

SORROW   **PAIN**

GUILT   **GRIEF**

These words imply that the emotions are simply too BIG for us to accommodate — that we don't have "enough room" for them.

NOW LET'S LOOK AT WHAT WE MEAN BY *EXPANSION*:

EXPAND: spread
unfold
develop.

BUT IF I OPEN UP TO MY FEELINGS THEY'LL TAKE OVER AND I'LL *LOSE CONTROL*!

THAT'S JUST YOUR MIND TELLING YOU *SCARY STORIES*! THANK IT AND MAKE ROOM FOR OTHER POSSIBILITIES.

BEFORE WE GO ANY FURTHER, LET'S REVISIT A VERY HELPFUL IDEA.

OH? WHAT IS IT?

REMEMBER THE TWO PARTS TO YOUR MIND, THE THINKING SELF AND OBSERVING SELF?

AH YES! CAN YOU REMIND ME AGAIN?

CERTAINLY ...

The **THINKING SELF** is
THOUGHTS
MOVEMENTS
IMAGES
MEMORIES

The **OBSERVING SELF** is
AWARENESS
ATTENTION
FOCUS

EXERCISE

Use your OBSERVING SELF to notice what is happening in your body and let your THOUGHTS come and go like a radio in the background.

Is your BREATHING SHALLOW? DEEP? FAST? SLOW?

How does your MOUTH feel? WARM? COOL? WET? DRY?

Position of ARMS?

Is there any tension in your NECK or SHOULDERS?

Do you feel HOT or COLD? WHERE do you feel this?

Is your SPINE STRAIGHT or BENT?

Position of LEGS?

How are your FEET placed?

Scan your whole body and notice any TENSION, PAIN, or DISCOMFORT.

Now notice any PLEASANT or COMFORTABLE sensations.

Do you feel like SHIFTING? Shift and notice how it feels.

Do you feel any urge to EAT, SLEEP, SCRATCH, STRETCH?

NOTICING your body is different to THINKING about it.

THINKING SELF gives the "commentary."

WHAT'S THE *POINT* OF THIS?

I HOPE I'M DOING IT *RIGHT*.

OBSERVING SELF just notices the sensations.

And sometimes, for brief moments when you are observing, the THINKING SELF shuts up!

In EXPANSION we sidestep our thoughts and connect with our emotions through the OBSERVING SELF. In doing so, we experience emotions as they are rather than as the THINKING SELF says they are i.e. we NOTICE rather than THINK.

When there is traffic outside your window you don't leap up to check every car! Likewise you don't have to respond to every THOUGHT!

But if a screeching tire distracts you, simply REFOCUS.

IN EXPANSION YOU LET THOUGHTS *COME AND GO* IN THE BACKGROUND AND KEEP YOUR *ATTENTION* ON THE *SENSATIONS* IN YOUR *BODY*.

REMEMBER:

▶ Emotions arise from PHYSICAL CHANGES in the body.

▶ Focus on their PHYSICAL SENSATIONS.

EXPANSION WITH PAINFUL EMOTIONS: 3 steps

1 **OBSERVE** Scan your body for uncomfortable feelings.

Are they STILL
or MOVING?

How DEEP
do they go?

Where are they
STRONGEST?
WEAKEST?

Where do they
START and END?

Find the sensation
that bothers you
most and observe
it with CURIOSITY
and OPENNESS.

2 **BREATHE**

SLOW, DEEP
BREATHS

Breathe directly
INTO and AROUND
sensations and make
ROOM for them.

It's as if you open
up and expand
AROUND the feelings.

3 **ALLOW**

THANKS
MIND!

EEK!!

Simply
acknowledge
any unhelpful
thoughts.

ALLOW the
sensations to be
there even if you
don't LIKE them.

Say "Thanks
mind" to any
RESISTANCE.

Don't try to GET RID OF the sensation or ALTER it. The goal is to see it as it is, and make PEACE with it. Focus on the sensation until you DROP THE STRUGGLE WITH IT. Then move onto another sensation until you are no longer fighting them.

By being WILLING to feel them they'll have less impact and influence over you.

BUT ISN'T THAT *MASOCHISTIC*?

ONLY IF IT SERVES NO *GOOD PURPOSE*!

SO WHAT'S THE *GOOD PURPOSE*?

IMPROVING YOUR *HEALTH* AND TO LEARN VALUABLE SKILLS TO *TRANSFORM YOUR LIFE*!

OKAY, I'LL *GIVE IT A GO*!

GOOD! SO BRING TO MIND SOMETHING THAT *DISTRESSES* YOU, GET IN TOUCH WITH A *PAINFUL FEELING*, AND PRACTICE THE 3 STEPS OF EXPANSION.

EXERCISE

Please practice the 3-step exercise described above, for 3 to 5 minutes, two or three times a day.

In the next chapter, we'll look at any difficulties you may encounter.

Chapter 9

Troubleshooting expansion

The concept of EXPANSION is simple but it's not EASY!
But like any meaningful challenge it's worth the effort.
Let's explore some of the difficulties you may encounter
in the beginning and troubleshoot them.

I TRIED MAKING
ROOM FOR THE
FEELINGS BUT
THEY WERE TOO
OVERWHELMING!

DON'T TRY TO TAKE
ON TOO MUCH.
JUST DO *ONE*
SENSATION FIRST
THEN THE NEXT.

WOW! THE
FEELINGS
DISAPPEARED!

ENJOY THAT WHEN
IT HAPPENS — BUT
REMEMBER, IT'S A *BONUS*,
NOT THE MAIN AIM.

I MADE *ROOM*
BUT THE
FEELINGS WERE
STILL THERE!

THEY WILL COME
AND STAY AND
GO IN THEIR
OWN GOOD TIME.

OKAY, I'VE MADE ROOM FOR MY FEELINGS, *NOW WHAT*?

NOW IT'S TIME TO TAKE EFFECTIVE ACTION IN LINE WITH YOUR *VALUES*.

WHY DO YOU KEEP COMING BACK TO *ACTION* AND *VALUES*?

TO CREATE A *RICH* AND *FULL* LIFE WE NEED TO ACT ON OUR VALUES (AS YOU'LL SEE LATER IN THIS BOOK).

IS SLOW, DEEP BREATHING ESSENTIAL?

NO, BUT IT'S HELPFUL. *OBSERVING* AND *ALLOWING* ARE KEY, THOUGH.

BUT WHEN I'M UPSET I JUST *GO NUMB*!

MAKE *ROOM* FOR YOUR NUMBNESS FIRST. YOU MAY FIND OTHER FEELINGS FOLLOW.

HOW CAN I DO THIS EXERCISE IF I'M AT WORK OR SOMEWHERE *PUBLIC*?

DO IT *QUICKLY*! TAKE A DEEP BREATH AND MAKE ROOM FOR THE FEELING. THEN ENGAGE IN THE TASK AT HAND.

CAN THE *THINKING SELF* HELP EXPANSION?

YES — WITH *SELF-TALK* AND *IMAGERY*.

EXPANSION SELF-TALK

I DON'T *LIKE* THIS FEELING BUT I HAVE *ROOM* FOR IT.

IT'S UNPLEASANT BUT I *ACCEPT* IT.

I'M HAVING THE *FEELING* OF ...

I DON'T *LIKE* IT OR *WANT* IT BUT I WON'T *FIGHT* IT.

EXPANSION IMAGERY

Scan for unpleasant feelings. Visualize the sensation as an object.

What size?
Shape?
Color?
Texture?
Fixed?
Shifting?

Now breathe into it and make room for it.

HOW MUCH *PRACTICE* DO I NEED TO DO?

AT LEAST *3 TIMES A DAY*, BUT THE MORE THE *BETTER*! TRAINING MAKES YOU SKILLFUL.

BUT ISN'T IT *UNHEALTHY* TO KEEP FOCUSING ON UNPLEASANT FEELINGS?

YES, IF YOU ARE *CONSTANTLY DWELLING* ON THEM BUT NOT IF YOU ARE LEARNING *EXPANSION SKILLS*.

The aim is to let your feelings come and stay and go without a STRUGGLE. Focus on them ONLY to practice expansion. Otherwise, focus on doing what you VALUE.

Chapter 10

Great connections

We've all "drifted off" at times.

The **THINKING SELF** has one job only: to generate thoughts. But sometimes these thoughts can be DISTRACTING.

This is how we habitually go through most of our lives!

How much do you give your FULL ATTENTION to:

EATING?   **WORKING?**   **READING?**

There are times when being absorbed in our thoughts ASSISTS what we are doing ...

But too often it DOESN'T.

We become DISCONNECTED. This is where CONNECTION comes in.

IT'S BEING FULLY PRESENT AND AWAKE IN THE *HERE* AND *NOW* AND BEING CURIOUS ABOUT AND OPEN TO WHATEVER IS HAPPENING.

WHAT'S THAT?

WHY IS THIS *IMPORTANT*?

SO YOU CAN ENGAGE *FULLY* IN LIFE.

TO FULLY APPRECIATE YOUR LIFE YOU NEED TO GIVE IT YOUR ATTENTION!

PAST

PRESENT

FUTURE

YOU COULD BE EATING THE MOST BEAUTIFUL MEAL OF YOUR LIFE BUT IF YOU'RE LOST IN YOUR THOUGHTS YOU'LL HARDLY EVEN *TASTE* IT.

WORK WAS *HELL* TODAY.

I HOPE I DON'T LOOK *GREEDY*!

WILL I GET THAT REPORT IN ON *TIME*?

As LEO TOLSTOY put it ...

THERE IS ONLY ONE TIME THAT IS IMPORTANT: **NOW!**

We can only ever take action here and now, and to take effective and valuable action we need to be fully present.

CONNECTION is:

▶ waking up

▶ noticing what's happening

▶ appreciating the fullness of every moment.

This comes NATURALLY in life's wonderful moments, but it's hard to do when life is DIFFICULT or PAINFUL!

Here's a comparison between **FUSION** and **CONNECTION**:

FUSION	**CONNECTION**	**FUSION**	**CONNECTION**
DISTRACTED	ENGAGED	JUDGMENTAL	DEFUSED FROM JUDGMENTS

WHAT'S OVER *THERE?*

This should be better

I shouldn't be like this

THIS IS WRONG!

FUSION	**CONNECTION**	**FUSION**
EASILY BORED, KNOWS IT ALL	CURIOUS & PRESENT	LIVES IN PAST OR FUTURE

BEEN THERE, DONE THAT!

IF ONLY   WHAT IF?

FUSION	**CONNECTION**	**THINKING SELF**	**OBSERVING SELF**
CLOSED OFF	OPEN	STRUGGLES AGAINST REALITY	NOTICES & OPENS TO REALITY

THIS SUCKS!

THIS CAN'T BE HAPPENING!

OKAY I'M *GAME.* WHAT DO I DO?

TRY THESE EXERCISES.

CONNECTION EXERCISES

GUIDELINES

If thoughts or feelings distract you:

- let them come and go
- bring back your attention when it wanders (and it will!)
- silently say "Thanks Mind."

1. Connection with ENVIRONMENT — 30 seconds

Put the book down and notice your SURROUNDINGS.

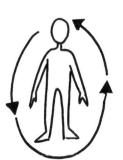

Use all your senses. Notice five things that you can:

HEAR
SEE
FEEL.

2. Awareness of your BODY — 30 seconds

Notice the POSITION of your whole BODY.

Do an internal scan and notice what you feel in EVERY PART.

3. Awareness of BREATH — 30 seconds

Connect with
your BREATHING.

Notice the FLOW
in and out.
Notice what your
body does with
the breath.

4. Awareness of SOUNDS — 30 seconds

What do
you HEAR?

SO, WHAT DID
YOU NOTICE?

I DIDN'T
REALIZE
THERE WAS SO
MUCH GOING
ON THAT I'D
MISSED!

WE ARE
SO EASILY
DISCONNECTED
AREN'T WE?

When we fuse with the stories our mind tells us, it keeps us DISCONNECTED from all that life offers.

The more we get caught up in unpleasant THOUGHTS and FEELINGS, the more we are cut off from what's ACTUALLY happening and our chance to engage with what we DO want.

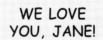

We can get hooked by
DOOM and GLOOM
about the FUTURE:

We can get hooked by
DOOM and GLOOM
about the PAST:

IT MIGHT
BE *AWFUL*!

I LOST
EVERYTHING!

It's hard to enjoy what
you're doing if you're not
connected with it, if you're
LOST IN THOUGHTS!

But the REVERSE is
also true!

THERE'S
NO POINT!

I'M
REALLY
INTO
THIS!

So CONNECTION is an important skill for getting the
MOST out of life.

EXERCISE: CONNECT WITH PLEASANT ACTIVITIES

Practice connection with at least one pleasant activity
each day.

EXERCISE: CONNECTION WITH A USEFUL CHORE

Pick a chore you don't like and practice connection.

- Have no EXPECTATIONS.
- Just NOTICE what you do.
- Open your SENSES to what's happening.
- If you feel boredom or frustration MAKE ROOM for it.
- If your attention wanders, thank your mind and REFOCUS.

EXERCISE: CONNECTION WITH A TASK YOU'VE BEEN AVOIDING

Pick a task you've been putting off.

Set aside 20 minutes and make a start on it with connection.

After 20 minutes you are free to stop or continue.

Do 20 minutes a day
till the task is completed.

Practicing connection is like building MUSCLES to strengthen your ability to handle change and move on with your life.

And important changes usually involve DISCOMFORT.

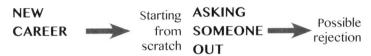

NEW CAREER ➡ Starting from scratch **ASKING SOMEONE OUT** ➡ Possible rejection

AVOIDANCE =
NO CHANGE/STUCK

CONNECTION =
MOVEMENT/IMPROVEMENT

AREN'T THE REWARDS *WORTH IT?*

You can CONNECT, DEFUSE, and EXPAND ... or NOT! The choice is yours.

Another word that describes a process of DEFUSION, EXPANSION, and CONNECTION is MINDFULNESS.

This is not about having a "FULL MIND"!

The *ACT* definition of MINDFULNESS would be:

▶ paying attention with openness and curiosity

▶ making room for whatever thoughts and feelings arise

▶ engaging fully in your here-and-now experience.

EXERCISE: MINDFUL BREATHING

Take six slow deep breaths. After a full out breath, breathe in gently. (If you're doing it right, your tummy will expand.) Practice connection: notice your breath flowing in and out!

> MINDFUL BREATHING
> IS A GOOD WAY
> TO PRACTICE YOUR
> MINDFULNESS SKILLS.

What did you notice?

> MY
> TENSION
> EASED.

> MINE
> DIDN'T!

> I
> STARTED
> "LETTING
> GO."

> I
> DIDN'T!

> I
> CONNECTED
> WITH MY
> BODY.

> I
> DIDN'T!

> MY
> MIND
> WENT
> QUIET.

> MINE
> DIDN'T!

> IF YOU DIDN'T FIND THE
> EXERCISE HELPFUL, PLEASE DO
> PERSIST. IF YOU PRACTICE IT
> FIVE TIMES A DAY FOR TWO
> WEEKS, YOU SHOULD START TO
> NOTICE THE BENEFITS.

MINDFUL BREATHING can connect you with the HERE and NOW.

THREE EXERCISES

Take 6 breaths again but for the first three focus on the BREATHING itself.  **CHEST ABDOMEN**

For the next three expand your focus to include your SURROUNDINGS.  **CHEST ABDOMEN**

What did you NOTICE?

Now do 9 breaths

First three: Focus on BREATHING.

Next three: Focus on BREATHING and THOUGHTS.

Last three: Focus on BREATHING and what you FEEL in your BODY.

This variation rapidly increases self-awareness, helps you accept thoughts and feelings, and gather your wits.

Now do 12 breaths

First three: Focus on BREATHING only.

Second three: Focus on BREATHING and THOUGHTS.

Third three: Focus on BREATHING and THOUGHTS and BODY.

Final three: A broad focus on BREATHING and THOUGHTS and BODY and the WORLD AROUND YOU.

NOTE: MINDFUL BREATHING IS NOT A *RELAXATION TECHNIQUE* OR A WAY TO *AVOID FEELINGS*. IT'S AN ANCHOR, TO HOLD YOU STEADY IN THE MIDST OF AN EMOTIONAL STORM.

REMEMBER — <u>ONE</u> SLOW, DEEP BREATH CAN HELP TO ANCHOR YOU UNTIL THE STORM PASSES.

Fancy a CHALLENGE?

EXERCISE

(Allow 10 minutes, once or twice a day.)

Sit or lie comfortably.

Let your thoughts come and go.

Focus on your breath for 6 minutes.

When your attention wanders, refocus.

For the next 3 minutes focus attention on your body, and its feelings and sensations.

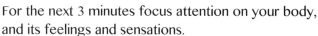

For the final minute open your eyes and take in the room around you.

Regular practice will bring noticeable PHYSICAL and PSYCHOLOGICAL benefits.

Chapter 11

You're not who you think you are

What do you most DISLIKE about yourself?

I'M TOO
SHY/
ANXIOUS/
NEEDY

STUPID
SILLY
DISORGANIZED

FAT
UGLY
UNFIT
LAZY

SELFISH
CRITICAL
VAIN

BORING
SERIOUS
DULL

JUDGMENTAL
AGGRESSIVE

UNDERACHIEVER
FAILURE, LOSER

WORKAHOLIC
CHOCAHOLIC
ALCOHOLIC

CONTROLLING
OBSESSIVE
FUSSY

These are only a few of the
most common responses.
The range is infinite but
there is one basic theme:

I'M NOT GOOD
ENOUGH AS
I AM!

No matter how hard we try or what we achieve, our
THINKING SELF always finds FAULT with us.

YOU MIGHT TELL YOURSELF *GOOD THINGS* ABOUT YOURSELF ...

I'M DOING WELL AT MY JOB. I EAT WELL, EXERCISE, I'M GENEROUS. THEREFORE I'M A *GOOD PERSON.*

AND IF YOU CAN TRULY *BELIEVE* THAT YOU ARE A GOOD PERSON YOU WILL FEEL GOOD.

BUT ALL TOO OFTEN YOU FIND YOURSELF HAVING TO *PROVE* OR *JUSTIFY* THIS POSITION ...

I'M GOOD ... ... AREN'T I?

... OR HAVING TO *DISPUTE* THE "NOT GOOD ENOUGH" STORIES THAT CREEP IN.

So like a game of chess, you find yourself constantly caught in a battle between GOOD and BAD thoughts and feelings.

I'M A NICE GUY.

I'M SELFISH.

You advance the "Good Guys" across the board ...

... only to find a whole army of "Bad Guys" waiting to counterattack.

Trying to feel good about yourself through positive AFFIRMATIONS will have LIMITED success ...

Firstly, you are unlikely to BELIEVE it any more than saying ...

... secondly, even if what you're saying rings TRUE ...

I'M A KIND AND CARING PERSON.

I'M LOYAL AND TRUSTWORTHY.

your **THINKING SELF** will still come up with negative counter-argument: this always happens.

WHAT ABOUT *THAT* TIME?

YOU DON'T *ALWAYS* KEEP SECRETS.

EXERCISE

Repeat the following statements to yourself and notice what thoughts pop into your head in response:

I am a human being.

I am a worthwhile human being.

I am a lovable, worthwhile human being.

I am a competent, lovable, worthwhile human being.

I am a perfect, competent, lovable, worthwhile human being.

YEAH, *RIGHT*!

WHO ARE YOU *KIDDING*?

STOP TALKING *RUBBISH*!

YOU *WISH*!

WHAT A JOKE!

Did you find the more POSITIVE the affirmation, the more NEGATIVELY your mind responded? Now let's REVERSE it and see what happens:

I AM A USELESS, WORTHLESS, UNVALUED PIECE OF HUMAN GARBAGE.

HANG ON A MINUTE: I'M NOT *THAT* BAD! NO WAY — I DON'T BELIEVE THAT!

The reality is we can waste a lot of time locked in this never-ending battle, which is often FIERCE.

HOW COULD YOU BE SUCH AN IDIOT?

YOU'RE NOT AN IDIOT. YOU JUST MADE A MISTAKE!

WHO ARE YOU KIDDING? LOOK AT LAST TIME.

BUT THIS TIME IS DIFFERENT! I'VE LEARNED MY LESSON.

YEAH RIGHT! YOU'LL ALWAYS STUFF IT UP!

NO I WON'T!

WILL TOO!

And while all your attention is on this BATTLE it's hard to connect with anything ELSE. You get lost in your thoughts instead of engaging in LIFE.

I'M A LOSER.

THANKS MIND! THERE'S THE *"I'M NOT GOOD ENOUGH"* STORY.

And if your mind tells you a POSITIVE story ...

I'M WONDERFUL!

THANKS MIND! THERE'S THE *"I AM GOOD ENOUGH"* STORY!

Let your mind chatter away like a radio in the background ...

... and engage fully in your LIFE.

After all, at your funeral, would you want your loved ones to be thinking something like this ...

SHE WAS SO CARING AND LOVING AND KIND AND GENUINE.

... or this?

SHE HAD A REALLY HIGH OPINION OF HERSELF.

You are not who you think you are. So unhook from the story, and get PRESENT!

AND REMEMBER: THERE ARE TWO ESSENTIALS FOR MAKING LIFE RICH, FULL, AND MEANINGFUL. ONE: *ENGAGE MINDFULLY* IN WHATEVER YOU ARE DOING. TWO: MAKE SURE WHAT YOU ARE DOING IS *MEANINGFUL*!

I KNOW HOW TO DO THE FIRST ONE, BUT HOW DO I DO THE SECOND?

YOU'LL FIND OUT IN THE NEXT PART OF THE BOOK.

Chapter 12

Follow your heart

In order to create a rich, full, and meaningful life, it's important to reflect on WHAT WE'RE DOING and WHY WE'RE DOING IT.

It's time to ask some BIG QUESTIONS in order to clarify your VALUES.

▶ What is deeply important to you?

▶ What sort of person do you want to be?

▶ What sort of relationships do you want to build?

▶ If you weren't struggling with feelings and avoiding fears what would you channel your time and energy into doing?

VALUES are:

▶ our heart's deepest desires for how we want to behave, and what we stand for in life

▶ how we want to treat ourselves, others, and the world around us.

When we live guided by values, we gain vitality and we experience life as RICH, FULL, and MEANINGFUL — yes, even when it HURTS.

VALUES are not the same as GOALS.

VALUE	GOAL
I WANT TO BE LOVING AND CARING.	*I WANT TO GET MARRIED.*

VALUE

▶ How you want to behave, deep in your heart.

▶ A direction you want to keep moving in.

▶ An ongoing process with no end.

GOAL

▶ Something you want to get, complete, have, own, or achieve.

▶ Once achieved, it's over and done with; completed; "ticked off the list."

GOAL	GOAL COMPLETED	WITH ONGOING VALUES	WITHOUT ONGOING VALUES
I WANT A BETTER JOB.	*YOU'RE HIRED.*	*I WANT TO BE PRODUCTIVE, CREATIVE, AND RESPONSIBLE.*	*I'LL SHOW UP TILL HOME TIME.*

WHY ARE VALUES SO *IMPORTANT?*

LET ME INTRODUCE THE JEWISH PSYCHIATRIST *VIKTOR FRANKL.*

Life can be HARD WORK. Anything meaningful brings CHALLENGES. Often this leads us to give up or quit.

IT'S *TOO HARD.*

I'M NOT EVEN *GOING THERE!*

VALUES make the EFFORT worthwhile.

If your values are:

CONNECTING WITH NATURE	**BEING A LOVING PARENT**	**SELF-CARE**

... you'll make the trek.	... you'll make time to play with your kids.	... you'll exercise and eat well.

But what if (like so many, not just those who are depressed) you think:

WHAT'S THE POINT?   IS THAT ALL THERE IS?   I HAVE NOTHING TO OFFER.   SOMETIMES I DON'T WANT TO LIVE ANYMORE.

Even THEN, values can give your life PURPOSE and MEANING.

EXERCISE

Imagine that you're 80 years old.

Now finish the following sentences:

▶ I spent too much time worrying about ...

▶ I spent too little time doing things such as ...

▶ If I could go back in time I would ...

NOW NOTICE — ARE THOSE *DEMONS* COMING BACK ON THE DECK OF THE BOAT?

YES!

THOUGHT DEMONS

I'm a hypocrite!
I'll fail!
It's too late!
I can't change!
I'm too busy!
I'm too tired!
I shouldn't have to!

FEELING DEMONS

Anxiety
Confusion
Guilt
Frustration
Fear
Shame
Regret
Embarrassment

SO DROP ANCHOR!

HOW?

UNHOOK FROM THE THOUGHTS. *MAKE ROOM* FOR THE FEELINGS AND GET *PRESENT*! IN OTHER WORDS: *DEFUSE*, *EXPAND*, AND *CONNECT*.

What do you really WANT?

These answers are not VALUES — they are all GOALS. To help you clarify VALUES, please do the exercise in the next chapter.

And remember: the PAST doesn't exist — it's just MEMORIES in the PRESENT ...

... and the FUTURE doesn't exist either — it's just THOUGHTS and IMAGES in the PRESENT.

Chapter 13

The 1000-mile journey

We're going to start this chapter a little differently to all the others: no cartoons, just an exercise on clarifying your values. Please complete it before reading the rest of the book; it's very important for everything that follows later.

EXERCISE: CLARIFY YOUR VALUES

Below are 40 of the most common values. Please read through the list and write a letter next to each value, based on how important it is to you:

V = very important

Q = quite important

N = not important

1. Acceptance/self-acceptance: to be accepting of myself, others, life, etc.

2. Adventure: to be adventurous; to actively explore novel or stimulating experiences

3. Assertiveness: to respectfully stand up for my rights and request what I want

4. Authenticity: to be authentic, genuine, and real; to be true to myself

5. Caring/self-care: to be caring toward myself, others, the environment, etc.

6. Compassion/self-compassion: to act kindly toward myself and others in pain

7. Connection: to engage fully in whatever I'm doing and be fully present with others

8. Contribution and generosity: to contribute, give, help, assist, or share ☐

9. Cooperation: to be cooperative and collaborative with others ☐

10. Courage: to be courageous or brave; to persist in the face of fear, threat, or difficulty ☐

11. Creativity: to be creative or innovative ☐

12. Curiosity: to be curious, open-minded, and interested; to explore and discover ☐

13. Encouragement: to encourage and reward behavior that I value in myself or others ☐

14. Excitement: to seek, create, and engage in activities that are exciting or stimulating ☐

15. Fairness and justice: to be fair and just to myself or others ☐

16. Fitness: to maintain or improve or look after my physical and mental health ☐

17. Flexibility: to adjust and adapt readily to changing circumstances ☐

18. Freedom and independence: to choose how I live and help others do likewise ☐

19. Friendliness: to be friendly, companionable, or agreeable toward others ☐

20. Forgiveness/self-forgiveness: to be forgiving toward myself or others

21. Fun and humor: to be fun loving; to seek, create, and engage in fun-filled activities

22. Gratitude: to be grateful for and appreciative of myself, others, and life

23. Honesty: to be honest, truthful, and sincere with myself and others

24. Industry: to be industrious, hardworking, and dedicated

25. Intimacy: to open up, reveal, and share myself, emotionally or physically

26. Kindness: to be kind, considerate, nurturing, or caring toward myself or others

27. Love: to act lovingly or affectionately toward myself or others

28. Mindfulness: to be open to, engaged in, and curious about the present moment

29. Order: to be orderly and organized

30. Persistence and commitment: to continue resolutely, despite problems or difficulties.

31. Respect/self-respect: to treat myself and others with care and consideration

32. Responsibility: to be responsible and accountable for my actions

33. Safety and protection: to secure, protect, or ensure my own safety or that of others

34. Sensuality and pleasure: to create or enjoy pleasurable and sensual experiences

35. Sexuality: to explore or express my sexuality

36. Skilfulness: to continually practice and improve my skills and apply myself fully

37. Supportiveness: to be supportive, helpful, and available to myself or others

38. Trust: to be trustworthy; to be loyal, faithful, sincere, and reliable

39. Other: ....
....
....
...

40. Other: ....
....
....
...

Adapted from *The Confidence Gap* by Russ Harris (Boston: Trumpeter, 2008).

SO I'VE IDENTIFIED MY *VALUES — NOW WHAT?*

NOW YOU NEED TO TAKE *ACTION!* A MEANINGFUL LIFE DOESN'T JUST *HAPPEN —* YOU NEED TO *MAKE* IT HAPPEN!

LET'S BEGIN BY DIVIDING YOUR LIFE INTO *FOUR DOMAINS:*

1. HEALTH

Includes physical health, psychological health, spiritual health.

2. LEISURE

Includes fun and games — relaxation, sports, hobbies, creativity.

3. WORK/EDUCATION

Includes unpaid work (e.g. volunteering) and apprenticeships and self-education (e.g. reading books).

4. RELATIONSHIPS

Includes friends, family, neighbors, co-workers, etc.

NOTE: Start with one domain at a time or you'll get overwhelmed and give up. Over time, you can work through all of them.

SO HOW DO I START?

THERE ARE FIVE STEPS IN SETTING MEANINGFUL GOALS:

STEP 1: SUMMARIZE YOUR VALUES

Write down four or five of the most important values in this domain ...

IN MY RELATIONSHIP WITH MY WIFE MY VALUES ARE *LOVE, CARING, HONESTY,* AND *SUPPORT.*

HEALTH — MY VALUES ARE *SELF-ENCOURAGEMENT* AND *SELF-COMPASSION.*

STEP 2: SET AN IMMEDIATE GOAL

Boost your confidence by starting with a SMALL, EASY goal — one that can be accomplished TODAY!

BE SPECIFIC

I'LL *RING* MY WIFE AND TELL HER I LOVE HER.

I'LL *WALK* FOR 10 MINUTES AT LUNCHTIME.

I'LL COOK A *HEALTHY* DINNER.

Remember: the journey of 1000 miles begins with a single step!

STEP 3: SET SOME SHORT-TERM GOALS

What are some small things you can do over the coming days or weeks that are consistent with your values?

I LIKE *HELPING OTHERS* BUT THIS JOB DOESN'T ALLOW IT ...

... SO I'LL SEARCH THE *INTERNET* FOR A MORE MEANINGFUL JOB.

Remember: lots of small steps ADD UP.

STEP 4: SET SOME MEDIUM-TERM GOALS

Now stretch yourself a bit further.
Remember: be SPECIFIC.

I VALUE TAKING CARE OF MY BODY — I'LL JOIN A *GYM* BY THE END OF THE MONTH.

I'LL COOK *HEALTHY RECIPES* THREE NIGHTS A WEEK.

I'LL TAKE A 20 MINUTE *WALK* EVERY DAY.

STEP 5: SET SOME LONG-TERM GOALS

WHAT
CHALLENGES
WILL TAKE ME
IN MY *VALUED
DIRECTION*?

WHAT WOULD
I LIKE TO DO
IN THE NEXT 6
MONTHS, 1 YEAR,
5 YEARS, ETC?

ACTION PLANS

Now break down your goals into an action plan.

▶ What smaller steps are required to complete this?

▶ What resources do I need?

▶ When, specifically, will I carry out these actions?

If your goal is to go to the gym three times a week your ACTION PLAN might be to:

Join the gym **Get your gear together** **Plan the times you'll go**

The RESOURCES you might need may be:

Money for membership ... **... gym gear** **... and a bag to put this in.**

Being SPECIFIC may involve:

You can:

- **change your goal**

- **make an ACTION PLAN to obtain the resources.**

Sometimes a resource is a SKILL:

MY GOAL IS
TO IMPROVE
RELATIONSHIPS
BUT I DON'T
KNOW *HOW*!

You can:

- **plan how you will learn the skill**
- **research/read, etc**.
- **take a course**.

EXERCISE

Write down:

- a domain of life to work on
- your values in that domain
- goals (immediate, short, medium, long-term)
- your action plan for the immediate and short-term goals.

The GOOD NEWS is ...

THE MOMENT YOU START STEERING
TOWARD THE SHORE YOU'RE NO LONGER
DRIFTING ALL AT SEA AND YOU CAN
MAKE THE MOST OF THE JOURNEY ALONG
THE WAY, KNOWING YOU'RE FINALLY
HEADING IN THE *RIGHT DIRECTION*!

Chapter 14

Finding fulfillment

IN A *VALUES-FOCUSED* LIFE YOU'RE MORE LIKELY TO ACHIEVE YOUR GOALS.

WHY?

BECAUSE IF YOUR *GOALS* ARE IN LINE WITH YOUR *VALUES*, YOU'RE MORE *MOTIVATED* TO PURSUE THEM!

PLUS — *CONNECTING WITH* AND *ACTING ON* YOUR VALUES CAN GIVE YOU FULFILLMENT RIGHT NOW.

IN WHAT WAY?

SAY YOU WANT TO BUY A HOUSE — THAT'S YOUR *GOAL* — BUT YOU CAN'T AFFORD IT YET. WHY WOULD YOU PURSUE THAT GOAL?

TO PROVIDE *SECURITY* AND *TAKE CARE OF* MY FAMILY.

SO TAKING CARE OF THE FAMILY IS THE *CORE VALUE* HERE, YES?

YES.

WELL YOU CAN TAKE CARE OF YOUR FAMILY *ANYWAY*!

I SEE! I CAN STILL LIVE TO MY *VALUES* WHETHER OR NOT I GET THE *HOUSE*!

IF YOU BELIEVE YOU CAN'T BE HAPPY TILL YOU'VE ACHIEVED YOUR GOAL, LIFE WILL BE *MISERABLE*!

BUT I REALLY *WANT* THE HOUSE!

YOU DON'T HAVE TO GIVE UP ON YOUR *GOAL*! START SAVING!

SO I DON'T HAVE TO WAIT TILL I GET THE HOUSE TO HAVE THE SATISFACTION OF CARING FOR MY FAMILY.

Let's look at some other examples:

I WANT TO BE A DOCTOR BUT IT'S TEN YEARS OF *HARD SLOG*!

What is the CORE VALUE of that GOAL?

I'LL BE ABLE TO *HELP PEOPLE*!

There are many ways you can do that RIGHT NOW!

A common GOAL is to find a PARTNER ...

SIGH, I'M *LONELY*!

... and to be MISERABLE if you HAVEN'T!

So what is the
CORE VALUE here?

TO BE *LOVING,*
CARING,
SENSUAL, AND
FUN!

You can still act on
those values with
FAMILY, FRIENDS —
and YOURSELF.

BUT THAT'S
NOT THE
SAME!

No it's not, but you have a CHOICE ...

▶ to find meaning, here and now, in living by your values
or

▶ to be miserable by focusing on a goal you haven't
achieved yet.

WHAT IF
I *ACHIEVE*
MY GOAL?

THERE'LL ALWAYS
BE *SOMETHING*
ELSE YOU WANT!

If you're always FOCUSED on GOALS, you will NEVER be
content. However, your VALUES are ALWAYS available.

Chapter 15

A life of plenty

A beneficial by-product of creating a meaningful life is that POSITIVE EXPERIENCES will happen.

ISN'T THAT A *GOOD* THING?

OF COURSE — AND IT MAKES SENSE TO APPRECIATE THESE THINGS TO THE FULLEST WHILE YOU'RE EXPERIENCING THEM ...

... BUT MAKING THEM THE MAIN *GOAL* IN LIFE IS NOT HELPFUL.

HOW COME?

Because you'll end up back in the HAPPINESS TRAP!

The more you focus on having only PLEASANT FEELINGS ...

... the more you'll STRUGGLE against the UNPLEASANT ones.

THEN WHAT SHOULD I *DO* ABOUT *PLEASANT* FEELINGS?

BRING *MINDFULNESS* TO THEM!

EVERY DAY IS FULL OF OPPORTUNITIES TO *APPRECIATE* YOUR LIFE, EVEN WHILE YOU'RE *IMPROVING* IT!

BUT WE USUALLY DON'T EVEN *NOTICE* THESE THINGS.

WITH *MINDFULNESS* YOU CAN WAKE UP & EXPERIENCE ALL AROUND YOU!

HOW DO I DO *THAT*?

HERE ARE SOME WAYS ...

When you EAT, slow down and SAVOR it.

TASTE it. Feel the SENSATIONS in your mouth.

If it RAINS, pay ATTENTION to it.

Hear the PITCH and VOLUME. Watch the PATTERNS it makes. SMELL the air.

When it's SUNNY, APPRECIATE it.

FEEL its WARMTH on your skin. See how everything BRIGHTENS.

• •

When you hug, kiss, or shake hands with someone, ENGAGE in it.

Notice how it feels. Let WARMTH and OPENNESS flow through you.

When you feel good, SAVOR it.

Notice how it feels in your BODY. Notice all the SENSATIONS, THOUGHTS, and IMAGES. APPRECIATE it.

Look into the eyes of a person you care about as if for the FIRST TIME.

OBSERVE everything about them — GESTURES, MOVEMENT, FEATURES.

Observe an ANIMAL with childlike CURIOSITY.

Take a familiar object and STUDY it as if you'd never seen such a thing before.

Before you get out of bed take TEN DEEP BREATHS.

See its COLORS, MOVEMENTS, CONTOURS.

Use all your SENSES, appreciate its FUNCTION.

Notice the MOVEMENT of your lungs and feel wonder at how they give you LIFE.

As you connect with your values and act in accordance with them you may notice changes in OTHERS, too.

The more you act like the person you WANT TO BE ...

... the more you'll notice POSITIVE RESPONSES toward you.

ENJOY these responses. Be MINDFUL. Notice what is happening and APPRECIATE it.

When you act with OPENNESS, KINDNESS, and ACCEPTANCE you'll probably receive the same ...

... MOST of the time!

(If not, go elsewhere!)

Savor POSITIVE INTERACTIONS and notice the ABUNDANCE in your life.

Build the CONNECTIONS by:

EXPRESSING what you appreciate about others, life, and yourself;	SHARING your difficulties and rewards;	LETTING OTHERS KNOW what they mean to you.

I LIKE THE WAY YOU DO THAT.

CAN I TELL YOU ABOUT...?

YOU'RE SUCH A *GOOD* FRIEND!

When you achieve goals that are in line with your values, there's often a pleasant emotion. Notice how it feels and ENJOY it — even the simple things.

THERE! IT'S *TIDY*.

A NICE, *HEALTHY* DINNER!

JUST A NOTE TO SAY HI!

It's all too easy to miss these things when the THINKING SELF tries to distract you with STORIES.

NOT GOOD ENOUGH!

MINDFULNESS

▶ awakens you to good things you may have taken for granted

▶ cultivates an attitude of openness and curiosity

▶ helps you to notice more opportunities

▶ provides stimulation and interest

▶ improves relationships

▶ increases fulfillment

▶ enables effective action.

NATURALLY IT'S EASIER TO BE MINDFUL WHEN LIFE IS GOING *SMOOTHLY.*

IN THE *TOUGH* TIMES, YOUR THOUGHTS WILL KEEP TRYING TO PULL YOU *OFF COURSE.*

THE IMPORTANT THING IS TO REMEMBER TO *PRACTICE* IT!

AND KEEP *CATCHING MYSELF* WHEN I GO OFF TRACK!

Chapter 16

Willingness

Say you've decided to climb a mountain because of the SPECTACULAR VIEW at the top.

Halfway up it's STEEP, NARROW, and ROCKY.

You're COLD, TIRED, and WET ...

... and you know it will only get WORSE.

I DIDN'T THINK IT WOULD BE *THIS* HARD!

But you're WILLING to endure this discomfort not because you WANT it or ENJOY it but because it's on the way to where you WANT to GO.

I'LL HAVE THE *SATISFACTION* OF MAKING IT AND SEEING THOSE *GREAT VIEWS*!

And say you want to write a book — you'll encounter many OBSTACLES ...

FUSION WITH UNPLEASANT THOUGHTS AND FEELINGS

I'LL NEVER SUCCEED.

WHAT IF I *FAIL*?

I'M NOT *GOOD* ENOUGH.

I FEEL *SCARED*.

PROCRASTINATION AND PUTTING OFF   or   **AVOIDANCE AND DISTRACTION**

THERE'S NO HURRY.

I CAN'T THINK ABOUT IT NOW.

I NEED A DRINK.

DEADLINE 1 WEEK!

You might finally
TAKE ACTION

OKAY —
I'LL SET A
MANAGEABLE
GOAL.

... and give it
MEANING ...

WHAT ARE MY
VALUES BEHIND
THIS GOAL?

... and acknowledge
that no matter
the outcome the
effort will be
WORTHWHILE.

JUST DOING THIS
WILL EXPAND MY
SKILLS.

But now you're
down to the NITTY
GRITTY and it's
getting HARDER.

I'M
BLOCKED.

You may be
tempted to BAIL
OUT ...

I'M REALLY NOT
ENJOYING THIS!

BUT I'LL
KEEP GOING!

... that's where
WILLINGNESS
comes in.

WILLINGNESS MEANS

▶ making room for unpleasant thoughts and feelings in order to do something meaningful

▶ getting out of your comfort zone to do something you value.

WILLINGNESS DOESN'T MEAN YOU **LIKE**, **WANT**, OR **APPROVE** OF UNPLEASANT THOUGHTS AND FEELINGS. IT MEANS YOU *ALLOW* THEM, SO YOU CAN DO WHAT MATTERS.

Willingness is something we practice in small ways every day ...

WHAT *THOUGHTS*, *FEELINGS*, *SENSATIONS*, AND *URGES* AM I WILLING TO HAVE IN ORDER TO DO WHAT I *VALUE*?

TIRED!

| To enjoy a movie you're willing to PAY for the ticket. | To go on holiday you are willing to PACK. | To pass an exam you're willing to STUDY. |

Willingness is the only way to deal with OBSTACLES. When an obstacle presents itself you can say:

NO!

and your life stays stuck or gets smaller ...

OR

YES!

in which case there's no guarantee that life will get easier ...

or that there won't be another tougher or bigger obstacle down the road!

But by saying YES your life will get BIGGER.

HOW WILL MY LIFE *EXPAND* IF I STILL KEEP MEETING OBSTACLES?

BY SAYING YES YOU GAIN EXPERIENCE AND INNER STRENGTH. YOU GROW AS A PERSON!

If FINDING A PARTNER is important to you, along the way you'll experience:

REGRET DOUBT ANXIETY

And you might have some real DISAPPOINTMENTS!

Either you're WILLING to go through this or you're NOT.

HE WAS WORTH IT.

• •

You might want to change to a more MEANINGFUL JOB ...

I WANTED *STATUS* AND *MONEY*. NOW I WANT TO *HELP* PEOPLE.

which might mean:

- less pay
- years of extra study
- parental disapproval.

But if you're WILLING you might reach your goal.

FRUSTRATION
NEGATIVE THOUGHTS
INSECURITY
DOUBT
VULNERABILITY
OLD "STORIES"

EXERCISE

Make a list of what you are willing to experience in order to reach your goal.

Now ask yourself:

ARE THERE
ANY OF
THESE
I CAN'T
HANDLE?

NO!

(provided you practice EXPANSION, DEFUSION, and CONNECTION)

WHAT
WOULD BE
USEFUL
REMINDERS?

WHAT'S THE
SMALLEST,
EASIEST STEP I
CAN BEGIN WITH?

AND
WHEN
WILL I
BEGIN?

NOW!

Chapter 17

A meaningful life

You can apply the **ACT** principles to ANY area of your life you'd like to improve:

HEALTH LEISURE   **WORK/**   **RELATIONSHIPS**

EDUCATION

Whatever you're doing, ENGAGE FULLY with it.

Whoever you're with be FULLY PRESENT for them.

When unhelpful thoughts arise DEFUSE them.

Whenever unpleasant feelings arise MAKE ROOM for them.

And whatever your values are be FAITHFUL to them.

THE *ACT* SERENITY CHALLENGE

Develop the courage to solve those problems that can be solved, the serenity to accept those problems that can't be solved, and the wisdom to know the difference.

Adapted from the "Serenity Prayer"

If your problems CAN be solved ...	If they CAN'T be solved ...	And be sure to practice CONNECTION.
SHORT OF CASH	DISABILITY	
		FOCUS *HERE* AND *NOW*

... take EFFECTIVE ACTION in line with your values.	... use DEFUSION, EXPANSION, and CONNECTION to help you ACCEPT this.	

You can either **ACCEPT** *or* **take EFFECTIVE ACTION** *or* **do both simultaneously**.

And as you take action, ENGAGE FULLY in what you're doing. Act on your VALUES and pay attention to the effect your actions are having.

Remember, too: the PAST doesn't exist; it's just MEMORIES in the PRESENT. And the FUTURE doesn't exist; it's just THOUGHTS in the PRESENT.

REMEMBER: LIFE *GIVES MOST* TO THOSE WHO MAKE THE *MOST* OF WHAT LIFE *GIVES*!

SO WHAT DOES THAT LEAVE YOU WITH?

NOW!

.